Backyard Scientist®

Series Two

by Jane Hoffman

Illustrated by Lanny Ostroff

The award winning Backyard Scientist series includes:

"The Original Backyard Scientist." This widely read and popular book was the author's first writing effort and features many of her most popular experiments for children ages 4 through 12 years. **"Backyard Scientist, Series One."** The author's second book of science experiments provides children ages 4 through 12 more fascinating and fun ways to explore the world of science. This book is a sequel to the first book and the beginning of a series of science books. **"Backyard Scientist, Series Three,"** teaches young scientists ages 4 through 12 about the living world with experiments in biology, physiology, entomology and more. **"Backyard Scientist, Series Four,"** is the author's fifth book in the award winning series. Containing exciting and stimulating experiments for scientists of all ages, it is excellent for classroom, group, family and individual scientific investigations.

Backyard Scientist, Series Two
Spring 1989
Published by Backyard Scientist/Jane Hoffman
P. O. Box 16966, Irvine, CA 92713
©1989 by Backyard Scientist/Jane Hoffman

0-9618663-2-2

TABLE OF CONTENTS

THE REVIEWS ARE IN ON BACKYARD SCIENTIST
WHAT EDUCATORS AND PARENTS ARE SAYING ABOUT THE BACKYARD SCIENTIST

"For the easiest and most enjoyable approach to science experiments, I recommend (The Backyard Scientist) by Jane Hoffman"

-- Mary Pride
The Teaching Home

"Her goal (is) to see the public school system adopt an ongoing, daily, hands-on science curriculum. No one can say that Jane Hoffman isn't doing her part to try to achieve this aim."

-- Nita Kurmins Gilson
The Christian Science Monitor

("Hoffman's) own curiosity and energy are a large part of the appeal of The Backyard Scientist. 'I believe that science makes a difference in the way a child learns.'"

--The Chicago Tribune

"Anyone who can read, or get an assistant to read, can have fun building the experiments described in The Backyard Scientist series and then have even more fun using (Hoffman's) experiments to explore science."

-- Paul Doherty, Ph.D.
Physicist/Teacher

"What makes these experiments special is their hands-on nature. A firm believer that science makes a difference in how a child learns, Hoffman encourages kids to think for themselves, to ask questions and to observe the world around them."

-- Science Books and Films

"All of the experiments have been pre-tested extensively with groups of children."

-- Curriculum Product News Magazine

"I believe that you have many of the answers to our problems with science education in the early grades."

– Mary Kohleman
National Science Foundation
Washington, DC

"There are a lot of good reasons why you should order the books, but if you need another one, just remember you're doing it for a worthy cause--your students."

--Teaching K-8 Magazine

"Popcorn, ice cubes and string are among the materials used in her experiments...most of which the children conduct themselves. But the main ingredient is the enthusiasm that Jane generates in the fledgling scientists!."

-- Women's Day Magazine

"...(Backyard Scientist series) is the best 'hands-on' experience a young reader can help him or herself to. Original and highly recommended for schools and home-teaching."

-- Children's Bookwatch

"As a teacher, I truly appreciated your book. It was well organized and easy to follow. The experience with a variety of scientific concepts has sparked further interest in several areas with many of the students. They have asked for more!"

-- Amy Korenack
Resource Teacher

"She makes science come alive."

-- Orange Coast Daily Pilot

"Backyard Scientest teaches children the art of thinking."

-- Anaheim Bulletin

"My mom is a teacher and thinks these books are the greatest"

-- Ryan, Age 5

"I loved the 'Backyard Scientist Series.' I like things I hadn't thought of doing by myself."

-- Chris, Age 7

"I loved the 'Backyard Scientist' books. They are so great."

- Thomas Age 8-1/2

"I tried your experiments with my students and they went wild with excitement."

-- First Grade Teacher, Illinois

"I really appreciate the clear instructions, simple to get household supplies, and the complete and easy to understand explanations. Thanks for these wonderful books."

-- Mrs. Getz, Home Schooling Mom

Welcome to the intriguing, mystifying and stimulating Backyard Scientist Laboratory. The laboratory features hands-on science experiments. Performing the experiments in this book will enhance your critical thinking skills and expose you to the fun and interesting world of scientific explorations. The experiments, while designed to be simple to perform, represent complex scientific principles to which we are exposed in our daily lives.

As soon as you begin experimenting, you become a *Backyard Scientist* working in the real world of scientific investigation. Your laboratory is wherever you are experimenting, be it in your backyard, kitchen or basement.

As a Backyard Scientist working in your laboratories, there are some very important guidelines you must follow:
1. **Always** work with an adult.
2. **Never** taste anything you are experimenting with except when instructed to do so in the experiment.
3. **Always** follow the Backyard Scientist directions in the experiment.
4. **Always** wash your hands with soap and warm water after you finish experimenting.
5. **Be a patient** scientist. Some experiments take longer than others before results can be observed.
6. Some experiments in this book use household chemicals that are poisons if swallowed. I have included cautions at the beginning of all experiments in which these types of chemicals are used.
7. If you have any questions about any of the experiments, write to me, Jane Hoffman, The Backyard Scientist, P.O. Box 16966, Irvine, CA 92713.

You are ready to start experimenting. Have fun! When you complete all of the experiments be sure to read how to get your Backyard Scientist Certificate and how to join the Backyard Scientist Club. Details are at the back of the book.

Happy Experimenting,

Jane Hoffman

Your Friend,
Jane Hoffman
The Backyard Scientist

The Subject Matter of this work is based on the scientific. The author is specific in directions, explanations and warnings. If what is written is disregarded, failure or complication may occur — just as is the case in the laboratory. In the instances where flammable or toxic chemicals are involved, explicit explanation and warnings are provided.

ANTACID EXPERIMENT

Do you know what happens when you drop an antacid tablet in water?

Try the following Backyard Scientist experiment to discover the answer.

Gather the following supplies:

6 antacid tablets, 2 small bottles in the shape of a small test tube (like the kind prescription drugs come in from the pharmacy, **be sure to wash thoroughly before using),** 1 eye dropper, water, 1 spoon, 6 pieces of tin foil cut into 4″ x 4″ squares, 1 hand magnifying lens, 1 small piece of black paper cut into a square 4″ x 4″, 1 pencil and paper.

CAUTION: *REMEMBER NEVER EAT OR DRINK ANYTHING YOU ARE EXPERIMENTING WITH.*

Start Experimenting.

1. Pick up one of the antacid tablets and examine it very carefully with the magnifying lens.
2. Take the pencil and paper and write down the properties of the antacid tablet (color, is it heavy or light, hard or soft); and what about smell and feel?
3. Now take a guess and write down what you think the antacid tablet is made of.

4. Take the piece of tin foil, the spoon, and one antacid tablet, and using the back of the spoon, crush the tablet. Now take the magnifying lens and examine the crushed antacid tablet. Compare it to the whole antacid tablet. Put the crushed antacid tablet aside for later use.

5. Take another whole antacid tablet and put it on the tin foil. Using your hands, break it into 4 pieces.

6. Take the bottle, eye dropper and have 1 small cup of water ready. Pick up one of the pieces of antacid tablet that you just broke and put the tablet into the bottle, then add 5 eyedroppers of water and observe. Write down on the paper what is happening. Also use the magnifying lens to observe carefully.
7. Take the other 3 pieces and plop them into the bottle and quickly add the rest of the water from the small cup. Put the palm of your hand over the opening of the bottle for two minutes. Also, use your hand magnifying lens for a close up look to see what reaction is happening inside the bottle. What are you observing? Now pick up the bottle and put your hand on the bottom. Is it hot or cold?
8. You may repeat this again if you like.
9. Take the black paper with the crushed up antacid tablet that you set aside earlier. Fill a small cup with water, and using the eyedropper, put one drop of water at a time onto the crushed up tablet and observe what is happening. Use your hand magnifying lens for a closer look.

Can you answer the following questions from your observations?

1. What did you list for your properties of the antacid tablet?
2. When you crushed up the tablet, were all the parts the same? Did you find any crystals? Do you know what that type antacid tablet is composed of?
3. When you put the antacid tablet in water and put your hand over the opening, can you describe what you were feeling? When you picked up the bottle was it the same temperature as when you started? Did a change occur in the temperature of the bottle? Why do you think this change occurred?

4. When you put the antacid tablet in water did you see something instantly happening?

Backyard Scientist solution to experiment.

Did you discover all the properties of the antacid tablet, its smell, feel, color, and weight (technically known as density)? The properties of a substance are the special qualities of something. Properties are determined by the ingredients of a substance. Did you discover by careful observation of the crushed up antacid tablet, that the tablet is composed of powder and crystals? The actual ingredients are listed on the wrapper. When you plopped the pieces of antacid tablet into the bottle and put your hand over the opening of the test tube, you felt the pressure from the gas being released from the antacid tablet. The mixing of the water with the antacid tablet caused a bubbling and fizzling effect. When you dropped the antacid tablet into the bottle with the water, a chemical change took place and the gas, carbon dioxide (CO_2), was released. CO_2 is the chemical symbol for the carbon dioxide molecule and means there are two oxygen atoms and one carbon atom in each molecule. Carbon dioxide is used in fire extinguishers to put out some kinds of fires. It is also used in soda pop to make them fizz. Dry ice is made from frozen carbon dioxide. When you held the bottom of the bottle it felt very cold, because the reaction of the antacid tablet with water uses energy in the form of heat. The energy is obtained from the water, and consequently the water cools.

This experiment is fun to do over and over again.

CORNSTARCH EXPERIMENT

Can you turn cornstarch into a green liquid?

Try the following Backyard Scientist experiment to discover the answer.

Gather the following supplies:

1 Box cornstarch, 1¾ cups water, 1 Tbsp. green food coloring and an 8″ or 9″ round bowl (see through if possible). A fish bowl works well for this experiment.

CAUTION: *REMEMBER NEVER EAT OR DRINK ANYTHING YOU ARE EXPERIMENTING WITH.*

Start Experimenting.

1. Mix the cornstarch, water and green food coloring together in the bowl. The best way is to mix it with your hands.
2. Continue mixing it all up until you have a smooth mixture.
3. Now make a fist with your hand and pound on the mixture.
4. Now feel the mixture with your hand.
5. Roll a portion of the mixture into a ball and put it into the palm of your hand. Watch it very closely.

Can you answer the following questions from your observations?

1. How did the cornstarch mixture feel when you pounded on it?
2. How did the cornstarch mixture feel when you touched it gently?
3. What happened to the cornstarch mixture after you put it into the palm of your hand?

Backyard Scientist solution to experiment.

If you touch the cornstarch mixture it is soft. If you pound on it it is hard. After you put the cornstarch mixture into your hands did you notice that within seconds it gets very soft and pliable? You can keep re-forming this unusual mixture.

The reason this mixture has so many properties is because the cornstarch is ground into a very fine powder and the starch molecules lay like little platelets. When you pound on it, these platelets line up and hold their rigid form. When you slowly pick it up or put your finger on it, it will eventually glob like a liquid.

Other fun activities to do with this unusual mixture are to describe the properties, invent things to do with it, and make other discoveries about the mixture. If the mixture starts to dry out just add some water to it. This mixture can keep for days just by adding a little water when the mixture gets too dry. When not using the cornstarch mixture, cover it with plastic to keep in the moisture.

EGG EXPERIMENT

Can you make the shell from a raw egg disappear and then bounce the egg?

Try the following Backyard Scientist experiment to discover the answer.

Gather the following supplies:

2 raw eggs still in their shells, 2 glass jars of the same size with mouths wider than the eggs, 2 covers to fit the jars, 1 bottle of white vinegar, paper, and pencil, and lots of patience since this experiment takes two weeks to complete.

CAUTION: *REMEMBER NEVER EAT OR DRINK ANYTHING YOU ARE EXPERIMENTING WITH.*

Start Experimenting.

1. On your paper write Day 1.
2. Take two eggs and feel them. Now make notes on your paper about how they feel.
3. Put one egg in each jar.
4. Fill both jars with enough vinegar to cover the eggs, and put the lids on.
5. Now watch the eggs for about ten minutes and note what is happening on your piece of paper under Day 1.
6. Check the eggs several times during the day, each time noting what is taking place. Be sure to wash your hands each time you touch the eggs.
7. On Day 2 look at your eggs. This time take the covers off and feel the eggs. How do they feel now compared to the first time you felt them? Write down your observations under Day 2. Now crack the shell of one of the eggs. Be sure to wash your hands. Leave the eggs alone until Day 3.
8. On Day 3 feel the eggs and write down how they feel now and what differences you observe in the egg with the crack in it compared to the egg without the crack in it. Write down your observations under Day 3. Be sure to wash your hands after feeling the eggs.
9. Follow the above procedure for days 4,5,6,7,8,9,10,11,12, and 13 and write down your observations each time. Be sure to wash your hands each time you check on the eggs.
10. On Day 14 empty the liquid from the jars into the sink, rinse the jars, and rinse off the eggs rubbing away the residue of grit. Now hold the eggs to the light. What do you see? Now roll the eggs gently and bounce them a little. What happened to the shell? Did the vinegar react with the shell?

Backyard Scientist solution to experiment.

When you first put the eggs into the vinegar solution, the shells covering the eggs were very hard. Each day the shells covering the eggs became softer and softer until there was no shell on either of the eggs. As the shell and the vinegar combined you saw tiny bubbles form on the shell. This told you that the acid from the vinegar was acting on the alkaline shell and slowly dissolving it.

Did you notice that the cracked egg grew slightly in size and the vinegar went into the crack and "cooked" the membrane under the shell so that it was as firm as a little balloon full of water, and you were able to bounce it? The cracked egg grew larger than the uncracked egg.

CRYSTAL EXPERIMENT

Can you form crystals on charcoal?

Try the following Backyard Scientist experiment to discover the answer.

CAUTION: The following experiment must be done under the supervision of an adult. This experiment requires the use of ammonia which is a *poison.* Never eat or drink anything with which you are experimenting. Have an adult measure the ammonia and pour it. Ammonia has a very strong smell and children should stand back when the ammonia is used in the experiment. Always use rubber gloves when working with ammonia. Avoid all close contact with skin, face, eyes and so on with the ammonia. *Keep the ammonia bottle tightly capped when not in use and always keep this and other poisons away from children's reach.*

Gather the following supplies:

1 glass pie plate, 1 old wooden spoon not used for food preparation, 6 charcoal briquettes broken up into small pieces (have an adult break the charcoal into small pieces—a hammer works well), 3 small household sponges cut into small pieces, 1 large jar with a lid, 6 Tbsp. *non-iodized* salt, 6 Tbsp. laundry bluing (ask your grocer if you don't spot this on the shelf, it is usually kept with the laundry detergents), 3 Tbsp. household ammonia (have an adult pour and measure this), red, orange, green, and blue food coloring, measuring spoons, something with which to spray water, lots of old newspapers to work on, 1 pair of old rubber gloves that are not used to touch food and a small lamp with 100 or 150 watt bulb (optional). ***Prepare this experiment in the garage or outside on an old table.***

Start Experimenting.

1. Take the newspaper and spread it out on an old table or the floor.
2. Put on the rubber gloves and gather the sponge pieces and charcoal and put them on the newspaper. Spray them with water until all the sponges and charcoal are saturated thoroughly with the water.
3. **With the rubber gloves on,** pick up the charcoal and sponge pieces and arrange these in piles in the pie plate.
4. Measure 3 Tbsp. only of the non-iodized salt and put it into the jar. Now measure the 6 Tbsp. of laundry bluing and pour that into the jar. Have an *ADULT measure the 3 Tbsp. of ammonia* and pour this into the jar. (Don't get too close to the ammonia while it is being poured.) Take the wooden spoon and stir this mixture until the salt has dissolved into the liquid.

5. Pour this mixture carefully into the pie plate dampening the charcoal and sponge pieces thoroughly. Now add 2 Tbsp. of water to the jar and mix it well with the leftover salt in the jar and pour this over the charcoal and sponges.
6. Take the blue food coloring and sprinkle drops of it in separate areas on the charcoal. Do the same thing with the other three colors.
7. Take the remaining 3 Tbsp. of salt and sprinkle this over the entire arrangement.

8

8. Place the pie plate in a warm room, away from food, where it can be observed, but *not disturbed,* for several days. If you have a small lamp you can put the lamp over the charcoal garden and this will speed up the forming of the crystals.
9. Each day, for two days, put 2 Tbsp. each of water, ammonia, and bluing, in the jar and very carefully pour the mixture in the bottom of the dish but not on the charcoal or sponges. Remember have an *ADULT* pour the ammonia into the jar using all the cautions listed previously.
10. This experiment can take from one day to three weeks so be a patient scientist. The time will depend on the temperature of the room where the charcoal garden is kept, as the temperature determines the time needed for crystals to form.

Can you answer the following questions from your observations?

1. What do you think will now happen to the charcoal and sponges?
2. Do crystals grow or form?
3. Why is the liquid important to the formation of crystals?
4. Why do you think it is necessary to add the liquid every day for two days to the charcoal arrangement?
5. What does the food coloring do?
6. Can crystals be found in diamonds or other precious stone jewelry?
7. Can you find crystals in rocks?
8. Is the room temperature important?

Backyard Scientist solution to experiment.

Crystals may begin to form on the charcoal within a few hours and continue to form for several days or up to 3 weeks. The dis-solved minerals in the charcoal move to the surface of the charcoal as the liquid evaporates and the mineral residue forms crystals. Liquid will continue to move to the surface of the newly formed crystals to form crystals on top of crystals. Crystals do not grow like plants, therefore light and water are not important to forming crystals on the charcoal. Crystals form better in warm conditions than in cold conditions. Crystals are delicate while they are forming. If moved they will break and will not re-form due to their weak structure. Touch a crystal after it is formed, and it will feel like a powder, and it will crumble like powder if moved. This experiment should be placed where it can be observed, but not disturbed, for several days. Did you discover that the crystals look like small colored mushrooms? Ammonia is needed because crystals grow best in an alkaline solution. Non-iodized salt is used because any trace of an element such as iodine inhibits the forming of crystals.

For a follow up activity to this experiment, you can look at some mineral crystals like diamonds or other precious or semi-precious stone jewelry. Some rocks when cracked open will reveal glittering bits of mica or quartz crystals. When minerals are dissolved in liquids, which then evaporate, or when minerals melt and cool slowly, they form into crystals. Each type of mineral forms into its own special crystal pattern.

Author's Note: You may also use the heat of the small lamp to speed up the process of forming crystals by shining the light directly on the charcoal garden. If your water is very hard (lots of dissolved minerals in it) you may have to use bottled water. But first, try the experiment with your regular water.

THE ATOM EXPERIMENT

Can you compare a splitting atom to a drop of liquid?

Try the following Backyard Scientist experiment to discover the answer.

Gather the following supplies:

A small water glass about 6 or 8 ounce size, rubbing alcohol, cooking oil, water, a spoon, a fork and a paper towel.

CAUTION: *REMEMBER NEVER EAT OR DRINK ANYTHING YOU ARE EXPERIMENTING WITH.*

Start Experimenting.

1. Fill the water glass about half full with rubbing alcohol.
2. Add enough water to fill the glass two-thirds full.
3. Stir the alcohol-water mixture with the spoon.
4. Wipe the spoon dry and fill it with cooking oil.
5. Carefully bring the spoon close to the surface of the alcohol-water mixture in the glass. Then gently tip the spoon over. A single blob of oil will slide into the glass. When the blob of oil slides into the glass it will change the blob of oil into an oil drop that hovers somewhere in the middle of the glass.
6. Now observe the drop in the middle of the glass.
7. Take the fork and carefully prod the drop apart. As you are doing this observe very carefully what is happening to the drop of oil.

Can you answer the following questions from your observations?

1. What similarities can you think of between the oil drop and an atom?
2. What happened to the oil when you took the fork and prodded the drop apart?
3. Can you describe the parts of an atom?

Backyard Scientist solution to experiment.

The forces that hold the oil drop together are similar to the forces that hold an atom together. When you took the fork and prodded the drop apart, did you notice that at first, the drop bulged, and then it tore apart into two perfectly round oil drops? The oil-drop "atom" will have split into two

smaller "atoms." The drop wouldn't split until it was critically deformed by the fork. Atoms behave in much the same way. They resist splitting until some action critically deforms them.

Did you know that everything in the world is made up of atoms? An atom is the smallest particle of an element that can exist alone or in combination. An atom has electrons and protons in and around it, and they attract each other (very similar to the north and south poles of magents).

The nucleus is the center of an atom. A proton is a very small particle that occurs in the nucleus of every atom and has a positive charge of electricity. Electrons are very small particles that have a negative charge of electricity and form the part of an atom outside of the nucleus.

THE YEAST EXPERIMENT

Can you blow up a balloon using sugar and yeast?

Try the following Backyard Scientist experiment to discover the answer.

Gather the following supplies:

1 pkg. of dry yeast, 2 Tbsp. sugar, ½ cup lukewarm water, measuring spoons, bottle with narrow opening (soft drink bottle works well), funnel, and a balloon.

Start Experimenting.

1. Stretch out the balloon. Blow up the balloon. Then let out the air.
2. Using the funnel put 2 Tbsp. of sugar and 1 Tbsp. of dry yeast and ½ cup of luke-warm water to the mixture in the bottle. Swirl the bottle gently to mix the materials.
3. Attach the balloon to the bottle by stretching the opening of the balloon over the top of the bottle.
4. Set the bottle aside undisturbed in a warm area for several hours.
5. Keep checking the bottle to observe what is happening.

Can you answer the following questions from your observations?

1. Is the balloon getting bigger?
2. What is making the balloon blow up? Is it the water, yeast or sugar?
3. What do you think will happen after several hours? Will the balloon continue to get bigger?
4. Do you know what yeast is used for?
5. Does yeast need light in order for it to grow?
6. From where does yeast get its energy?

Backyard Scientist solution to experiment.

When yeast comes to life and starts growing, it gives off gas. Gas bubbles rise up out of the mixture. They cause the balloon to expand. The gas it gives off is carbon dioxide, which is composed of carbon and oxygen. Plants, through photosynthesis, give off oxygen, replenishing our supply of this vital element. Animals, through metabolism, is the process by which a living organism uses food to obtain energy, build tissue, and dispose of waste material using oxygen and giving off carbon dioxide.

The yeast that makes bread rise is a living organism that requires sugar, moisture, and warmth to grow. Yeast is a single-cell plant and is used in making bread and some alcoholic beverages.

Yeast has some rather unique characteristics. Unilke most of the plants that we are familiar with, yeast makes no food of its own and needs no light to survive and grow. The energy necessary for yeast's growth and metabolism must come from other foods already available. Yeast is very specific in the kind of food it can use. Yeast gets its energy from sugar. You might also try this experiment using other sweets such as honey, molasses and fruit juices. You can also try putting one experiment in light and the other experiment in the dark and see which balloon gets bigger.

COLOR CHANGE

Can you change the color of ink with the electricity contained in a battery?

Try the following Backyard Scientist experiment to discover the answer.

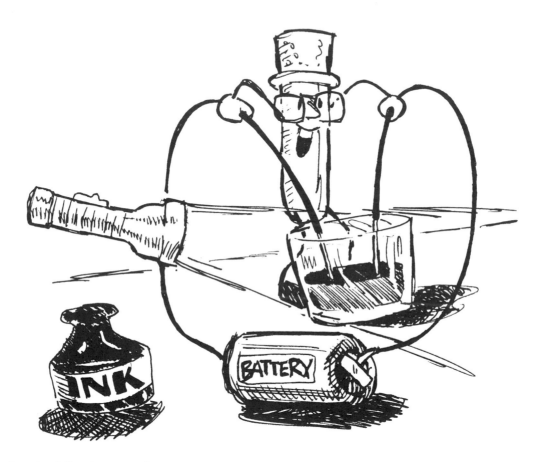

Gather the following supplies:

1 nine-volt transistor radio battery, 2 pieces of bell or other thin copper wire cut 21" long, 4 Tsp. of non-iodized salt, one 8 oz. glass, a small plastic or glass dish, 1 large piece of tin foil, pencil and paper, 1 flashlight, 1 roll of tape, 1 spoon and 1 bottle of blue ink (this can be obtained from a stationery store).

CAUTION: *REMEMBER NEVER EAT OR DRINK ANYTHING YOU ARE EXPERIMENTING WITH.*

Start Experimenting.

1. Fill the glass with water.
2. Add 1 Tsp. of salt to the water and stir. Then, slowly add the remaining salt to the water until no more can be dissolved. Keep stirring all the time. You are making a saturated solution.
3. Pour ¼ cup of this solution into the small plastic or glass dish.
4. Put the piece of tin foil on the table so you don't make a mess. Put the battery, wire, and dish with water all on the piece of tin foil. Take the two pieces of wire and uncover about 1½″ of bare wire at each end of the two pieces of wire.
5. Take the battery and connect a piece of wire to each terminal on the battery. Tape will hold the wires to the terminals on the battery.
6. Take the ink and put a drop or two into the small bowl with the ¼ cup solution in it. Stir to mix.
7. Place the other two ends of the bare wires, already attached to the battery, into the salt-ink solution. Be careful not to touch the two bare wires together. You will cause a short circuit if you do. Keep both wires pointed down in the solution for 5 minutes. Observe what is happening very carefully. If you are not in very bright light, take the flashlight and point it directly into the bowl so that you will be able to see more clearly what is taking place.

Can you answer the following questions from your observations?

1. Do you see bubbles forming at the end of each wire?
2. Do you know what these bubbles are?
3. Do you think the same kind of bubbles are forming at the negative wire and at the positive wire?
4. What color was the ink when you first put it into the water-salt solution?
5. Is the solution now the same color or different colors?
6. What do you think is making the ink change colors?
7. Do you think a chemical reaction or a physical change is taking place?

Backyard Scientist solution to experiment.

You saw bubbles forming at the end of both the negative and positive wires. The color of the blue ink changes into several different shades. The bubbles you saw forming at the end of the negative wire are tiny amounts of sodium hydroxide. Chloride ions are formed at the positive wire, and these react with water to form HClO, which will not hold together. It breaks up into HCl, hydrogen chloride and a very active form of oxygen we call ''nascent'' oxygen. The nascent oxygen is searching for another element or substance to combine with, and the ink colors are its victims. It destroys them.

With very small currents of electricity the chlorine is consumed by reaction with the copper wire or ink. With higher current, both chlorine and oxygen are produced at the positive electrode. The sodium hydroxide also can attack and destroy ink color. You have discovered a simple way that you can produce complex chemical reactions.

Author's Note: I tried several blue inks and Sanford so far has worked the best for this experiment.

JET PLANE

Do you know how a jet plane gets the power to fly?

Try the following Backyard Scientist experiment to discover the answer.

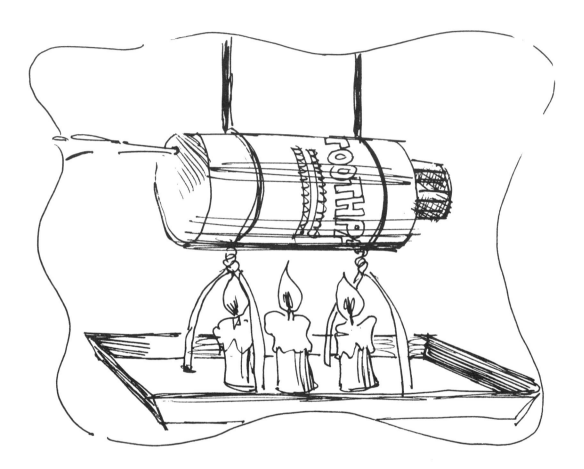

Gather the following supplies:

1 10 oz. toothpowder can with cap, ⅓ cup of water, matches, an aluminum cake pan, three short fat candles that can stand up by themselves (see picture), 2 pieces of stiff wire 12″ long, a nail and a hammer.

CAUTION: THIS EXPERIMENT REQUIRES ADULT SUPERVISION AND HELP.

Start Experimenting.

PLEASE PERFORM THIS EXPERIMENT IN THE BATHROOM AS YOU WILL BE USING THE BATHTUB AT THE END OF THE EXPERIMENT.

1. You are about to build a simulation of a jet plane to see how it gets its energy.
2. Get an adult to help you punch a small hole in the bottom of the can.
3. The two wires are going to be the stand for your jet. Take the two wires and twist each wire around the toothpowder can, making the legs for the jet. Make sure the legs are high enough for you to get the three candles underneath the can.
4. Take the can and fill it with ⅓ cup of water and put the cap back on. Then put 2″ of water in the bathtub.
5. Take the cake pan and set it in the bathtub.
6. Take the three candles and set them into the cake pan.
7. Have an adult light the candles and put the toothpowder can over the lighted candles.
8. Let the water inside the can get hot and watch what happens.

Can you answer the following questions from your observations?

1. When the water in the can was heated, what did the water become?
2. Do you know what steam is?
3. Did the pressure of the steam build up in the can?
4. How did the steam escape from the jet you built?
5. Do you know now how a jet plane works?
6. Does a propeller driven airplane work the same way a jet plane does?

7. Does a jet plane need air to fly?
8. Does a propeller airplane need air to fly?

Backyard Scientist solution to experiment.

A regular propeller airplane needs air to push back under and over its wings in order to lift the plane and fly forward. The water in the can was heated to the point where it changed into steam. Steam is a hot gas and builds up a lot of pressure. When contained, this pressure has to escape. In this case the pressure escapes through the tiny hole in the can. As the pressure is escaping, it is pushing the can forward. This is how a jet plane works. The hot gases from burning fuel are formed inside the engine, and when they shoot out at the rear they push the jet forward allowing air to flow over and under its wings giving lift.

RADIO WAVES

Is there any material that stops radio waves?

Try the following Backyard Scientist experiment to discover the answer.

Gather the following supplies:

1 transistor radio, a metal pot with a lid, wax paper, a large plastic bag, aluminum foil, large paper bag, large jar, large empty metal can, big cardboard box, a blanket, and a pencil and paper.

Start Experimenting.

1. Turn on the radio and put it into the pot with the lid. Can you still hear the radio? Write down your observations on the piece of paper.
2. Now take the radio (still on) and put it into the large paper bag. Can you still hear the radio? Write down your observations on the piece of paper.
3. Take the radio, still on, and test it with the other materials to see whether they stop radio waves. Be sure to write down your observations.

Can you answer the following questions from your observations?

1. Which of the objects tested stopped the radio waves from coming through?
2. Which of the objects tested let the radio waves pass through?
3. What are the materials made of that let the radio waves pass through?
4. Do you know what one kind of radiant energy is?
5. Can you explain what radio waves are and how they are produced? Can you think of another form of radiant energy?
6. Can we see radiant energy? Do you think visible light is a form of radiant energy?
7. How do the voices and music produced at the radio station get into your homes?

Backyard Scientist solution to experiment.

You will discover the materials that do not stop radio waves are the large jar, large paper bag, big cardboard box and blanket. The materials that stop radio waves are the metal pot with lid, aluminum foil and the empty metal can. Certain materials made out of metal will stop radio waves. Most materials that are not made out of metal will not stop radio waves.

The music and voices you hear are converted at the radio station into an electric current that moves back and forth in a wire. The current must move back and forth changing directions in the wire very fast, as often as one-half to one million times a second. The transmitter then changes the current into radio waves that can be sent into the air. These radio waves reach your radio by an antenna at the station that sends out radio waves in all directions. Your radio is a receiver because it changes radio waves back into current, and the current is sent to the speaker which vibrates to make the sounds you hear.

The development of the radio was one of the greatest advances in technology. The first long-distance radio transmitter was built by Guglielmo Marconi in 1901.

Radiant energy is produced when an atom absorbs energy, becomes excited, and releases radiant energy in tiny bundles called photons. One kind of radiant energy is radio waves. The only kind of radiant energy that we can see is visible light. To further explore the subject of radiant energy go to your library and discover all the different forms of radiant energy. It is a fascinating subject.

CAR EXPERIMENT

If you were racing two toy cars and you used automobile oil on one car and vegetable oil on the other car, which car would go the longest distance?

Try the following Backyard Scientist experiment to discover the answer.

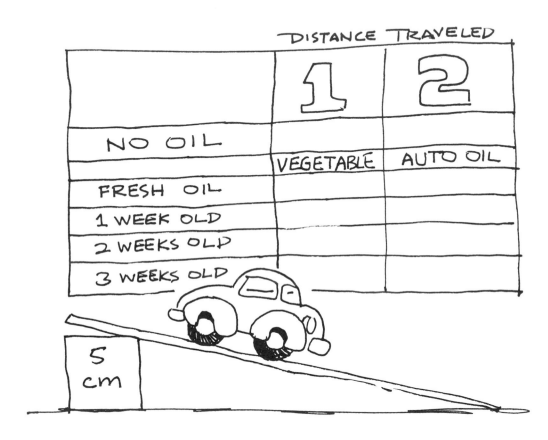

Gather the following supplies:

¼ cup of vegetable oil (safflower, corn, peanut, etc.), ¼ cup of #20 or #30 automobile oil, 2 small toy cars (such as hot wheels or match box cars), 1 tape measure, 1 wooden board (about 5″ wide), and a cardboard box (about 3″ tall).

Start Experimenting.

1. Take the wooden board and prop it on top of the cardboard box (like an inclined plane).
2. Label one of the cars No. 1 and the other car No. 2. Make a chart like the drawing on the opposite page.
3. Put each of the cars on the inclined plane starting at the top and let them roll down. Measure the distance each travels with the tape measure. Record the results under "no oil" on your chart.
4. Now add the vegetable oil to the wheels of the #1 car and the automobile oil to the wheels of the #2 car.
5. Now start each car on top of the inclined plane and let them roll down and measure the distance the cars traveled with the tape measure. Record your results under the vegetable oil column and auto oil columns on your chart.
6. Each week, for three weeks, test the cars without adding any more oil to the wheels. Record your results each time in the correct weekly column.

Can you answer the following questions from your observations?

1. Which of the cars traveled the farthest distance?
2. What differences did you observe in "oiled" cars each week?
3. Do you know where the energy originally came from which produced both cooking oil and automobile oil?
4. How does oil protect iron?
5. If you were a race car driver, what type of oil would you use based on your observations over the past three weeks?
6. Do you think oil is used in making paint? If so what kind of oil is used?

Backyard Scientist solution to experiment.

Automobile oil is a stable material that retains its lubricating properties for a long time. Cooking oil is unsaturated, which means it combines readily with the oxygen in the air. This tends to thicken and solidify the oil.

Since vegetable oil forms a solid film when exposed to air, it is used in paint. Special chemicals are added to the paint to speed up this process. Although adding anti-oxidants to vegetable oil slows the solidification process, it is not a good automobile lubricant. High engine temperature will break down the vegetable oil.

The energy that originally produced both the cooking oil and the automobile oil came from the sun.

BALLOON EXPERIMENT

Can you get a balloon that is blown up inside a small 8 ounce bottle?

Try the following Backyard Scientist experiment to discover the answer.

Gather the following supplies:

1 small bottle (soft drink bottles are great for this), a balloon, scissors, two small bowls, pot holders and hot and cold water.

Start Experimenting.

1. Cut the neck off the balloon. Stretch the top of the balloon a few times and set it aside.
2. Fill the bottle with hot water from the hot water tap and let it sit for about five minutes, then pour out the water. Use the pot holders.
3. Take the empty bottle and pull the balloon over the top of the bottle.
4. Take a bowl and fill it with hot water from the tap.
5. Stand the bottle in the bowl of hot water until the balloon is inflated just a little. Leave it in the hot water and go onto step 6.
6. Take the other bowl and fill it with cold water from the tap.
7. Put on the pot holders so you won't burn yourself. Take the bottle out of the bowl of hot water and carefully stand it in the cold water.
8. Now watch very carefully for the next five minutes. What is happening to the balloon? Where is it going? If you listen as well as watch carefully, you can hear what is happening.
9. How do you think the balloon got into the bottle?
10. Do you know a way to get the balloon out of the bottle without touching the balloon?
11. Take the bowl with the hot water and pour it out and put fresh hot water from the tap into it.
12. Take the bottle from the cold water and stand the bottle in the bowl of hot water.
13. Watch very carefully for about five minutes. What is happening to the balloon now?

Backyard Scientist solution to experiment.

When you warm the bottle with hot water, the air in the bottle is warmed. When air is warmed it expands and becomes less dense. When you cool the bottle with cold water, the air in it is cooled and contracts and becomes more dense. The cold air has less pressure than the warmer air outside the bottle. As the air inside contracts, the warmer air with more pressure outside pushes the balloon into the bottle filling the space left by the contracting molecules. If you warm up the bottle again, the air inside expands, increasing in pressure, and pushes the balloon out again.

DID YOU KNOW?

If you have a ping-pong ball with a dent in it, you can get it out. Put the ball in warm water. The air inside will expand and push out the dent.

A hot-air balloon floats up when the burner under the balloon heats the air in the balloon. This is because the heated air expands forcing out the cold air and expands the balloon. As there is less actual air in the balloon, it is lighter than the air in the surrounding atmosphere.

ELECTRIC QUESTION & ANSWER BOARD

Can you make a truth detector?

Try the following Backyard Scientist experiment to discover the answer.

Gather the following supplies:

1 cardboard shoe box lid, 20 feet of bell wire, 1 lantern battery with screw connections, a 6 volt light bulb (called "lamp") and 1 socket for the light bulb (this can be obtained from a Radio Shack or hardware store), 2 paper clips, scissors, a screwdriver, white paper, a pencil and a ruler.

Start Experimenting.

1. On the bottom of lid do the following: with the ruler and the pencil, mark off 10 places down the right side of the cardboard. Keep the spaces between the marks equal. Make a small hole in the cardboard at each mark. Number the holes from 1 to 10.

24

2. Make 10 more holes down the left side of the cardboard, directly across from the first 10. Number these holes, starting at the top, in this order: 9,7,5,1,4,6,8,2,10,3. This will be the back of the quiz board.
3. Now cut 13 pieces of wire, 15 inches long. Uncover 1 inch of bare wire at each end of all 13 pieces. Stretch the first wire between the two holes numbered "1." Put the ends of the wire through the holes. Turn the board over to the front. Twist the bare wire sticking through each hole into a loop to keep it from sliding out. Connect all the other pairs of holes in the same way. Make sure you connect matching numbers.
4. Now take 3 more pieces of wire, using one of them to connect the battery to the socket, by wrapping one end of the wire around one of the screws on the battery and the other end around one of the screws on the socket. Use the screwdriver to loosen and tighten the screws on the socket.
5. Take another piece of wire and connect this in the same way as you just did above; only this time connect the wire to the other screw on the battery, leaving the other end of this wire free.
6. Take another piece of wire and connect this to the other screw on the socket, leaving the other end of the wire free.
7. You might have extra wire left over which you can save in case you need to replace one of the wires on the box top.
8. Now cut a sheet of white paper to fit on the front side of the board between the wire loops.
9. Write 10 questions down the left side of the paper next to each wire loop. Write the answers to the questions down the right-hand side of the paper in this order: answers 9,7,5,1,4,6,8,2,10, and 3. Do not number the answers.
10. Clip the paper to the front of the board.
11. If you touch one of the free wires to the loop next to question 1 and the other free wire to the loop next to the answer to question 1, the bulb will light up. But if you touch one free wire to question 1 and the other free wire to any other answer, the bulb will not light up. You have to match the questions with the correct answers to make the bulb light up.

Can you answer the following questions from your observations?

1. Do you know why the light bulb lights when you match the question with the correct answer?
2. Do you know why the light bulb does not light when you match the question with the wrong answer?

Backyard Scientist solution to experiment.

The reason the light lit when you matched the question with the correct answer is because you completed the electric circuit. To create electricity you must have a complete circuit or path, this was accomplished by the electricity flowing through the wires. The light will not go on when you match the question with a wrong answer because you did not complete the electric circuit to that wire; therefore electricity did not flow through the incomplete circuit.

Trivia questions are fun to write on your electric quiz board. You can make up your own trivia game with several different sheets of questions and have teams playing against each other.

MAGNET AND PIN EXPERIMENT

Do you think you can make a pin float in air?

Try the following Backyard Scientist experiment to discover the answer.

Gather the following supplies:

1 straight pin (make sure the pin is attracted to the magnet), 1 student magnet (can be purchased from Radio Shack stores for about 21¢), 1 piece of black thread about 16″ long, and 1 unsharpened pencil.

Start Experimenting.

1. Tie one end of the thread to the head of the straight pin.
2. Tie the other end of the thread around the middle of the pencil.
3. Stick the magnet on metal, such as table legs or desk legs.
4. Touch the pointed end of the pin to the magnet. The pencil should rest on the floor.
5. Slowly pull the thread a few inches away from the magnet and the pin will "float" freely in the air. This does take practice and patience.

Can you answer the following questions from your observations?

1. Why do you think the pin is floating in air?
2. What is the pin made of that you used?
3. Do you think pins made out of materials other than iron or steel will float in air?
4. What other different ideas can you think of to do that will overcome gravity?
5. Can you think of any animals that can overcome the force of gravity?
6. Can you think of any way that you work against gravity?

Backyard Scientist solution to experiment.

The force of a magnet can work against the force of gravity. In the above experiment, the force of the small magnet was used to make the pin float in air, thereby temporarily overcoming gravity. Gravity pulls on all things, while magnets only pull on certain metals like iron and steel. Did you know that every time you jump up in the air your muscles help you to temporarily overcome the force of gravity, but then in a few seconds you come back down? When you jump off a diving board, gravity brings you down instead of allowing you to continue up. When you are walking, you are working against the pull of gravity.

Most animals and plants overcome the force of gravity to some extent.

Gravity is a force that cannot be seen, but it pulls everything toward the center of the earth. Try lifting something a little bit heavier than you are. Do you notice how hard it is to lift? This is because gravity pulls it down. The more an object weighs, the more gravity pulls on it. The gravity of the earth holds things on the earth. Weigh yourself on a scale. Your weight tells you how much gravity pulls on you.

For further studies into gravity, you might go to the library. Find out about how gravity would affect you if you lived on one of the nine planets or the moon. You might research how much you would weigh on the different planets.

RUSTING

Do you know which liquids cause iron to rust the fastest?

Try the following Backyard Scientist experiment to discover the answer.

Gather the following supplies:

4 plastic cups (4 or 5 ounces), or 4 clean small jars (the kind baby food comes in), 4 steel nails, vinegar, water, lemon juice, hydrogen peroxide, a measuring cup and pencil and paper.

CAUTION: *REMEMBER NEVER DRINK OR EAT ANYTHING YOU ARE EXPERIMENTING WITH.*

Start Experimenting.

1. Label the four jars or cups as follows: No. 1, hydrogen peroxide; No. 2, lemon juice; No. 3, water and No. 4, vinegar.
2. Pour ¾ of a cup of hydrogen peroxide into cup No. 1, ¾ cup of lemon juice into cup No. 2, ¾ cup of water into cup No. 3, and ¾ cup of vinegar into cup No. 4.
3. Drop a steel nail into each jar, making sure the entire nail is in the solution. Note: Steel nails are made from iron.
4. Now check the nails once a day for the next five days, and write down your observations each time you check them.

Can you answer the following questions from your observations?

1. Did you notice any change in any of the nails after the first day?
2. Do you know what makes steel rust?
3. Do you think the rusting of the steel has anything to do with which kind of liquid the steel is in?
4. What other things can you think of that might contribute to the rusting of the steel?
5. Did rust form on all the nails?
6. Which liquids caused the nail to rust the most?
7. Which liquids caused the least rusting?
8. Did any of the liquids change color?
9. Do you know what color rust is?
10. Can you name any processes that keep iron from rusting?

Backyard Scientist solution to experiment.

Did you observe that the nail that was in water rusted within a day? There was no change in the other nails. Atoms of most elements can combine to form compounds.

Rusting takes place when oxygen molecules are removed from the air or in this case the water, and combine with the iron of the nail. When the oxygen molecules leave the water the nail rusts. Because the nail is iron, the iron joins with oxygen from the water and together they form a different substance called iron oxide (rust). Rust is different from iron or oxygen. It is a brittle solid that crumbles and cannot be used for anything. Moist iron rusts more quickly than dry iron.

In summing up we can say that when a piece of uncoated iron is exposed to air and moisture, the iron changes into a red substance called rust, which is not at all like the original metal. This type of change is called a chemical change because the substance you started off with is no longer the same substance you ended up with. The process of milk becoming sour, the decay of fruit and burning of a match are other common and familiar chemical changes.

Fifty years ago many of the items that people used were made from an iron called cast iron. It was not satisfactory for many purposes. Steel is much better because it is stronger. Today much of the iron used is in the form of steel. Steel is made by adding carbon and other materials to iron and heat treating the mixture. It might be fun to go to the library and research other processes to keep iron and steel from rusting and to find out how these processes work.

COPPER

Can you copper plate a steel nail using vinegar and pennies?

Try the following Backyard Scientist experiment to discover the answer.

Gather the following supplies:

1 6 oz. plastic cup, 16 dull pennies, 1 Tbsp. salt, 1 new steel nail, 1 plastic spoon, 1 cup of vinegar, 1 small piece of paper towel, and a pencil and paper.

CAUTION: *REMEMBER NEVER TO DRINK OR EAT ANYTHING YOU ARE EXPERIMENTING WITH.*

Start Experimenting.

1. Take the plastic cup and put the pennies into it.
2. Fill the cup with vinegar.
3. Put 1 Tbsp. of salt into this solution.
4. Take the spoon and swish the pennies around a few times until they are all clean and shiny.
5. Take the steel nail and wrap it in the paper towel and put it into the vinegar solution.
6. Leave the nail in the solution for at least 8 hours. Check on it every hour and note on the paper what changes are taking place.

Can you answer the following questions from your observations?

1. Do you think the nail will change in color?
2. How did the copper get on the nail?
3. Is this change in the nail a chemical or physical change?
4. What does wrapping the nail in the paper towel have to do with this experiment?

Backyard Scientist solution to experiment.

When you wrapped the nail in the paper towel and put it into the solution, the paper towel acted as a wick and carried the copper and salt solution to the nail. Did you look at the nail after an hour and notice that the bottom of the nail was covered with copper? After eight hours, the whole nail will be covered with a bright coat of copper. What has happened is that some of the iron went into the solution and caused the copper to come out of the solution.

A physical change has taken place. Physical change is when a material changes in some way, but the molecules themselves stay the same. For instance, if you tear a piece of paper it is still paper, but now you have two pieces instead of one. The material is still the same. When different molecules form, a chemical change takes place. Burning is one kind of chemical change. When paper burns, it changes to a substance different from what it was. It changes into a black or gray ash substance. The molecules that made up the paper have been through a chemical change. A chemical change takes place when new substances form. These new substances may be seen if they do not go into the air as invisible gases.

SOUND EXPERIMENT

Can you build a musical instrument from a coat hanger?

Try the following Backyard Scientist experiment to discover the answer.

Gather the following supplies:

1 metal coat hanger, 2 pieces of black thread about 12" long, 2 paper or plastic small cups (2 or 4 ounces), one sharpened pencil, 2 paper clips and a partner to experiment with you.

Start Experimenting.

1. Take the coat hanger and tie the threads to each corner of the coat hanger.
2. Take the 2 cups and make a small hole in the bottom of each cup with the pencil.
3. Put the thread through the hole in the bottom of each cup pulling it through the hole. Then tie the thread around the paper clip in the inside of the cup.

4. Turn the coat hanger upside down and pull the cups to your ears.
5. Then tap the hanger against a table and listen carefully. Have your partner hold the thread while tapping the hanger against the table and listen again, then release thread.

6. Have your partner strike the hanger with the pencil in different places on the hanger while you listen. Repeat this with only one cup to your ear and listen again. Do not touch hanger during the experiment.
7. Now change places with your partner and repeat all lines 4 to 6.

Can you answer the following questions from your observations?

1. When you tapped the coat hanger against the table did you hear a sound? Do you know what caused the sound you heard?
2. When your partner held the string as you tapped the hanger against the table did you hear any sound?
3. Did you hear sounds when your partner tapped the hanger with the pencil in different places on the hanger? Did the sound change as the pencil tapped against the different places on the hanger?
4. What changes occurred when you removed one cup from your ear?

Backyard Scientist solution to experiment.

When you tapped the hanger against the table you heard a symphony with overtones and vibrations in stereophonic sound that no one else could hear but you. When your partner held the thread and you tapped the hanger against the table you heard no sound at all, because in order to have sound something has to vibrate and by holding the thread the transmission of the vibration was stopped. When the hanger was tapped with the pencil in different places the sound vibrated in many different wave lengths.

The various vibrations produced the sound which traveled from the vibrating metal hanger through the thread into the cups which produced the sounds that you heard with your ears. The vibrating thread causes the air in your ear to vibrate and produce the sounds you hear with your brain. Stereophonic sound is sound heard from the two cups. When you removed one of the cups from your ear, you lost the stereo sound because now the sound is one, coming from only one location instead of two.

Sounds can travel through solids, liquids and gases. Sounds travel best through solids. Vibrating objects produce sounds. The slower an object vibrates the lower the sound, while the faster it vibrates the higher the pitch of the sound. Did you know that when you talk you make vibrations? The air moving past your vocal chords in your throat produces sounds. The tongue, teeth and lips help to form these sounds into words.

For further investigations with the metal coat hanger, you can change the shape of the hanger by opening it and bending it and do the same experiments as above and see if there are any changes in the sounds you hear. Then you can make a list of different objects to strike the hanger with, and you can tape record the different sounds you hear. You can use different kinds of materials to thread into the cups like string, elastic, wool and so on to observe which material will best conduct sound or pitch. Can you think of other musical instruments you can make? Research music and sound in the library.

M & M

Can you do a science experiment with M & M Candies?

Try the following Backyard Scientist experiment to discover the answer.

Gather the following supplies:

1 pkg. of plain M & M Candies, an eyedropper, 1 sheet of newspaper, two large plastic plates, 1 plastic spoon, 1 scissors, one 4 oz. cup filled with water, and paper and pencil for notes.

CAUTION: *REMEMBER NEVER TO EAT OR DRINK ANYTHING YOU ARE EXPERIMENTING WITH.*

Start Experimenting.

1. Take the sheet of newspaper and with scissors cut the blank bottom strip of the newspaper into one long strip. Take the long strip and cut it in half.
2. From the M & M Candies take 2 red candies, 2 yellow candies, 2 green candies, 2 light brown candies and 2 dark brown candies.
3. Take the two yellow candies, the two green candies, the two light brown candies, and put them into a pile on one of the plates.
4. Take the small cup with water in it and the eyedropper and put ten drops onto the candies in the plate. Now take the spoon and swish the candies all around until most of the candy coating is removed from them. Now throw away the candy and take one of the strips of paper and dip one of the ends of the strip into the liquid from the candies and lay it over the plate.
5. Now take the two red candies and the two dark brown candies and repeat step 4 using the other plastic plate.
6. Leave this alone for a couple of hours and make notes on what is happening to the strips of paper on the two plates.

Can you answer the following questions from your observations?

1. What is happening to the liquid on the strips?
2. Is it one color or is it separating into many colors?
3. What are the colored chemicals in the candies being absorbed by?
4. Do you know the chemical name for separating chemicals like this?

5. Are the chemicals in the liquid absorbed at the same rates or at different rates?

Backyard Scientist solution to experiment.

The colored chemicals in the candies are being absorbed by the strips of newspaper in the same way as the chemicals in ink are absorbed by paper. They are absorbed at different rates, and as the chemicals separate you can see the different colors. Separating chemicals like this, by absorbing them, is called "chromatography."

Now try this same experiment, only this time change the colors of the candies around. See if you get different colors on the strips of paper. Compare these results with the original combination of colors. You can also do this same experiment using different colors of felt tip pens and making dots at the ends of the strips of newspaper and laying one end in a drop of water and watching the colors separate in this way. Try different kinds of paper too. Will the rate of absorption change?

PERISCOPE EXPERIMENT

Do you know what a periscope is? Let's build one.

Try the following Backyard Scientist experiment to discover the answer.

Gather the following supplies:

1 empty quart size milk carton, a knife to cut a hole in the carton, 2 pocket mirrors and some masking tape.

CAUTION: ADULT *SUPERVISION* AND HELP IS REQUIRED ON THIS EXPERIMENT. REMEMBER *KNIVES* ARE SHARP AND CAN CUT, SO BE VERY CAREFUL WHEN USING ONE.

Start Experimenting.

1. Have an adult help you cut a hole on one side of the milk carton near the top (make the hole just big enough for your eye to see through).
2. Have an adult help you cut a similar hole on the opposite side of the milk carton making it the same distance from the bottom as the other hole is from the top (just big enough for your eye to see through).
3. Have an adult help you tape the two pocket mirrors in place, parallel to one another. The mirrors should be at a 45-degree slant.
4. Hold the box up to your eye and discover what you see when you look through the lower hole.
5. Go to a corner and hold the box so that one hole is sticking out past the corner as you look through the other hole. What do you see?

Can you answer the following questions from your observations?

1. What were you able to see with the periscope that you can't see normally without it?
2. Have you figured out what makes a periscope work?
3. What do you think is one major use of periscopes?

Backyard Scientist solution to experiment.

Did you discover that you were able to see what is above you and on the opposite side of the box? The periscope also lets you see around corners. This is all possible because light is reflected by the mirror on top of the periscope to the mirror on the bottom of the periscope. If you look through the eyepiece at one end you can see objects reflected by the mirror at the other end.

Periscopes are used in submarines to see above water. In some parts of the world, theaters are equipped with periscopes so you can see the stage even if the person in front is taller than you.

MOLD

Do you know how mold grows?

Try the following Backyard Scientist experiment to discover the answer.

Gather the following supplies:

2 clear plastic cups (6 or 8 oz. size), plastic wrap to cover both cups, 1 hand magnifying lens, water, half a slice of bread, 1 slice of any citrus fruit with skin attached (grapefruit or orange), an eyedropper and a pencil and paper.

CAUTION: *REMEMBER NEVER TO DRINK OR EAT ANYTHING YOU ARE EXPERIMENTING WITH.*

Start Experimenting.

1. Take the two plastic cups and place the bread into one cup and the fruit into the other cup.
2. Take the eyedropper and add 10 drops of water to each of the two cups with the fruit and bread inside.
3. Keep the cups uncovered for one day in a warm place.

4. Cover the cups with plastic wrap. Place the cups in a warm place, out of the sunlight, where they will not be disturbed.
5. Observe the cups everyday without removing the plastic wrap. This investigation can take up to two weeks. Everyday write down if the mold has started to grow.
6. Keep observing until your pieces of food are covered with mold.
7. When your investigation is over, *DO NOT OPEN THE CUPS,* BUT *THROW* EVERYTHING AWAY IN A SEALED PLASTIC GARBAGE BAG.

Can you answer the following questions from your observations?

1. Do you think all molds that grow look the same?
2. Why is it important to keep the cups sealed when you get rid of the food with the mold on them?
3. Do you think if left long enough, all the food in the cups would disappear?
4. Where did the mold come from? What do you think is needed to grow molds and bacteria?
5. Take the hand magnifying lens and examine each piece of food through the plastic wrap. Write down or draw the descriptions of the different molds that are on the food.
6. How do you think Penicillin was discovered?

Backyard Scientist solution to experiment.

A common mold that grows on citrus fruits is Penicillin. It is grayish green with some white fuzz around the edges. The molds that grow on fruit are a kind of fungi. Fungi cannot make their own food. A fungi can feed on both plant and animal foods. The mold on the piece of bread grows through the bread taking food from it. It forms tiny black balls, called spore cases. Each spore case is full of spores. A spore is a living cell that can grow to become another mold. When the spore cases break open, the spores are carried through the air and settle on other food. As they grow, they make the food spoil. Bread mold feeds on wheat and other grains from which bread is made. If you leave the bread out long enough it will disappear, and all you will see is the mold, because the bread provided the substances which were needed by the mold for its growth. The molds in these investigations used the food for their growth. You might want to investigate the other kinds of molds and decay. It is a fascinating subject.

Molds and bacteria need a source of food, moisture, and a mild temperature in order to grow well. Room temperature is usually the best for growth. Molds don't grow well in direct sunlight. It is very important to keep the food covered and not to touch or eat any of it. Molds can spread to other materials or humans. Try experimenting with other kinds of food and see what kind of molds you can grow using the same procedures.

Dr. Sir Alexander Fleming proved that Penicillin produces a substance that kills some kinds of bacteria. Other scientists before Sir Alexander had suspected that molds produced such substances to kill some kinds of bacteria, but Sir Alexander designed the experiment which proved that the substances secreted by some molds would destroy certain bacteria. Further study would be to read about Sir Alexander's investigation that led to this wonderful discovery that saved so many lives.

INDICATOR EXPERIMENT

Can you make an indicator out of a laxative pill?

Try the following Backyard Scientist experiment to discover the answer.

Gather the following supplies:

1 laxative pill (from drug store), 1 saucer, 1 teaspoon, ¾ cup rubbing alcohol, 1 eyedropper, a small plastic bottle (3 or 4 oz. size with screw-on cap — the kind they sell at beauty supply stores), a funnel, 2 bowls and a bar of white soap.

CAUTION: *REMEMBER NEVER TO DRINK OR EAT ANYTHING YOU ARE EXPERIMENTING WITH.*

Start Experimenting.

1. Measure ¾ cup of alcohol and put this into the bowl.
2. Take one of the laxative pills, put it on the saucer and crush it with the back of the teaspoon.
3. Crush it as finely as you can, and mix it with the alcohol in the bowl. Let this mixture settle for a few minutes. You have made a test solution called phenolphthalein which is used as an indicator.
4. Transfer this solution from the bowl using the funnel, and pour the mixture into the plastic bottle. It is very important to label all chemicals. Label this Phenolphthalein Solution.
5. Take the bar of soap and put it into a bowl with ½ cup of water; using the eyedropper, take two drops of phenolphthalein and put it onto the soap. Observe what change is taking place.

Can you answer the following questions from your observations?

1. Did the white soap change to another color when you put the phenolphthalein on it?
2. Do you know what an indicator is?
3. Is the soap an acid or a base?
4. If you put the phenolphthalein on other substances, will it also turn them all bright pink?
5. Can you make a list of acids and bases?

Backyard Scientist solution to experiment.

The correct way to *pronounce* phenolphthalein is (feen-ole-they-leen, the middle ''ph'' is silent). Phenolphthalein is an indicator. It indicates or shows something. This solution indicates the presence of alkalis or bases by turning pink. Phenolphthalein in the presence of a base (like ammonia) turns red.

Alkalis or bases are bitter chemicals often found in kitchens and the laundry. MOST BASES SHOULD *NEVER BE TASTED.* MANY ARE DANGEROUS POISONS. Bases often have a soapy, slippery feel on the skin.

You can make a list of items to be tested. Label one side of your list acids and the other side bases. Ideas for substances to test are: baking soda, baking powder, different kinds of soaps, perfume, powders, shaving cream, cream of tartar, milk, orange juice, lemon juice, toothpaste, oil, and cleanser. What other items can you think of to test? Be sure to ask an adult for permission to use items to test to make sure there is nothing *poisonous or dangerous* that you are testing. Save the test solution. You will be using it in the next experiment.

SPECIAL NOTE:

AFTER DOING CHEMICAL EXPERIMENTS EVERYTHING SHOULD BE POURED DOWN THE SINK AND YOUR HANDS *WASHED* WITH SOAP AND WATER.

AUTHOR'S NOTE:

The laxative pill I use for this experiment is Feenamint.

RED WATER

Can you turn clear water into red water and then back to clear water again?

Try the following Backyard Scientist experiment to discover the answer.

Gather the following supplies:

4 tall clear glasses, one see-through pitcher, water, the phenolphthalein test solution you made in the previous experiment, eyedropper, 3 Tbsp. of white vinegar, teaspoon measure, tablespoon measure, 1 Tbsp. of ammonia, labels, and a marking pen.

CAUTION: THE FOLLOWING EXPERIMENT MUST BE DONE UNDER THE SUPERVISION OF AN ADULT. THIS EXPERIMENT REQUIRES THE USE OF AMMONIA WHICH IS A POISON. NEVER EAT OR DRINK ANYTHING YOU ARE EXPERIMENTING WITH. HAVE AN ADULT MEASURE THE AMMONIA AND POUR IT. AMMONIA HAS A VERY STRONG SMELL AND CHILDREN SHOULD STAND BACK WHEN THE AMMONIA IS USED IN THIS EXPERIMENT. ALWAYS USE RUBBER GLOVES WHEN WORKING WITH AMMONIA. AVOID ALL CLOSE CONTACT WITH SKIN, FACE AND EYES. KEEP THE AMMONIA BOTTLE TIGHTLY CAPPED WHEN NOT IN USE AND ALWAYS KEEP THIS AND OTHER POISONS AWAY FROM CHILDREN'S REACH.

Start Experimenting.

1. Take the four glasses and label them No. 1, No. 2, No. 3, No. 4.
2. Fill the pitcher with enough water to fill the four glasses and add 1 Tbsp. of ammonia to the clear water in the pitcher.
3. To glass No. 1 add 10 drops of phenolphthalein test solution.
4. Glass No. 2 is to be left empty.
5. To glass No. 3 add 10 drops of phenolphthalein test solution.
6. To glass No. 4 add 3 Tbsp. of vinegar.
7. Fill each glass with water from the pitcher and observe what is happening.
8. Pour the contents of the first, second and third glass back into the pitcher leaving the fourth glass with the water and vinegar still in it. Observe what is happening.
9. Now refill glass Nos. 1, 2, and 3 with the liquid from the pitcher.
10. Now pour the contents of all four glasses into the pitcher very slowly starting with the No. 1 glass, then the No. 2 glass, then the No. 3 glass, then the No. 4 glass.
11. Fill all the glasses again and observe what is happening.

Can you answer the following questions from your observations?

1. What color was the water in the first three glasses when you first poured it?
2. What color was the water when you poured the first three glasses into the pitcher?
3. When you refilled the glasses what color were the first three glasses of water?
4. Why do you think the fourth glass is always clear?
5. When you finally poured all the glasses back into the pitcher what color was the water in the pitcher?
6. How did it turn from red to white?

Backyard Scientist solution to experiment.

Remember you learned in the previous experiment that phenolphthalein is an indicator. It indicates or shows something. This solution indicates the presence of alkalis or bases by turning pink. Phenolphthalein in the presence of a base like ammonia turns red. With acids like vinegar it remains colorless. When the vinegar is in excess, the ammonia is neutralized and the phenolphthalein remains colorless *(AMMONIA IS A POISON — ALWAYS HAVE AN ADULT POUR AND USE THE AMMONIA)*. Many combinations of chemicals will bring about change.

After doing chemical experiments, everything should be poured down the sink, and your hands washed with soap and water as in the previous experiment.

IODINE

Can you turn a white piece of paper blue without using blue coloring or dye?

Try the following Backyard Scientist experiment to discover the answer.

Gather the following supplies:

2 Tbsp. cornstarch, water, toothpicks, tin foil, measuring spoons and cups, bowl, spoon, shallow pan, white paper, 1 large bottle of iodine or 2 small bottles, a pair of rubber gloves, and a plastic 6 or 8 oz. cup.

CAUTION: REMEMBER NEVER DRINK OR EAT ANYTHING YOU ARE EXPERIMENTING WITH. *IODINE IS A POISON.*

Start Experimenting.

1. In the bowl, mix together 1 Tbsp. of cornstarch with 2 Tbsp. of water. Stir with the spoon until the mixture is smooth.

2. Dip a toothpick into the cornstarch and water solution. Using the toothpick as a pen, draw a picture on the white piece of paper.

Special Note: In the next instruction you will be pouring iodine. When pouring iodine be very careful not to spill any, as it will stain *anything* **it touches. Work with the iodine over the sink. Take out the iodine rod very slowly and hold the rod against the bottle. The iodine will then run down the rod and go exactly where you want it to go.**

3. While your picture is drying, put on the rubber gloves and mix 1 Tbsp. of iodine with 1 cup of water in the shallow pan.
4. When your picture is completely dry, look at it. Is the picture very clear?
5. Still wearing the rubber gloves, dip the paper into the iodine mixture. Make sure the picture is completely covered by the solution. Keep it in the solution for about 1 minute.
6. Take the picture out of the iodine solution and put it onto a piece of tin foil to dry.
7. Now still wearing the rubber gloves, fill the glass with water and put 1 Tbsp. of iodine into it (be sure to follow the directions again for pouring under special note above) and observe what changes are taking place.

Can you answer the following questions from your observations?

1. Was your picture very clear before you put it into the iodine solution?
2. What color did your paper turn when you put it into the iodine solution?
3. Was the paper the same shade all over?
4. Why do you think the paper turned the color it did?
5. What do you think this test tells you about cornstarch?
6. Do you know what the sugars and starches in food are known as?
7. Do you know what this ingredient in bread, cornstarch, and some vegetables is that reacts with iodine?
8. Why didn't the water with the iodine turn a shade of blue?

Backyard Scientist solution to experiment.

Did you notice that your picture was not too clear until you put the picture into the iodine solution? The reason the paper turned dark blue is because iodine will combine with starch to form a new compound. Iodine is reddish-orange (as you saw when you put the iodine into the glass of water), starch is white, the new compound is dark blue. In this case the iodine combined with the starches in both the paper and the corn-starch mixture. There are different kinds and amounts of starches in the paper and the cornstarch. Therefore, they did not turn the same shade of blue when they reacted with the iodine.

Did you know that any food that turns blue-black when iodine touches it has starch in it? Chemists use this test to detect which foods have starch in them. If you put a drop of iodine on a potato, it will turn blue-black because a potato is full of starch. It might be fun for you to test different foods in the kitchen to see which contain starch. You can make a chart and record your results. **REMEMBER, IODINE IS A POISON, SO NEVER EAT OR DRINK ANYTHING THAT YOU ARE EXPERIMENTING WITH, UNLESS THE INSTRUCTIONS TELL YOU TO DO SO.** Always wash your hands with soap and water after each experiment.

Sugar and starches in foods are known as carbohydrates. Carbohydrates are an important part of your daily diet. Carbohydrates give you energy. You need energy to work and play. You get energy most easily from foods rich in carbohydrates. Before major sports events athletes eat large amounts of carbohydrates.

Starch is a white, odorless granular or powdery complex carbohydrate. Starch is an important food stuff. Starch is also used in adhesives, sizes in laundering and in pharmacy and medicine.

ICE

Will all objects sink into a block of ice?

Try the following Backyard Scientist experiment to discover the answer.

Gather the following supplies:

1 oblong dish with sides 1½" or 2" deep, several pennies, 3 nickels, 10 metal washers, 3 thumb tacks, 1 piece of chalk broken into small pieces, 4 small pieces of wood (2"x2") and a piece of paper and a pencil.

Start Experimenting.

1. Make an ice block by filling the oblong dish with water and putting the dish into the freezer. This should be left in the freezer overnight.
2. The next day gather the rest of the supplies and make a list of them on a piece of paper. Now make a prediction as to which objects will sink into the ice and which objects will not. Write down your predictions. After the experiment you will compare your predictions to the actual results of your experiment.

3. Take the block of ice from the freezer. Allow warm water to run over the *outside* of the dish for a few moments. This will loosen the block of ice and enable you to remove the ice from the dish.
4. Take the block of ice and put it on a table or flat surface.
5. Take all of the objects and place them one by one on the block of ice, observing what is happening. Write down your observations. Are the objects sinking into the ice?
6. Try pushing the washers into the ice.
7. Try putting the thumb tacks into the ice with their sharp ends down.
8. Can you get the penny to go all the way through the ice?
9. Try putting the washers into the ice while on their edges.
10. Look very closely at the nickel through the ice and observe what it looks like.

Can you answer the following questions from your observations?

1. Did the penny leave its impression on the ice?
2. Did you see Lincoln's face on the penny in the ice?
3. By pushing on the washer did the washer go in further?
4. Can you get a penny to go all the way through the ice?
5. What did the nickel look like to you when you examined it very closely through the ice?
6. Does the washer sink into the ice further when it is on its edge than when it is flat?
7. Does the thumb tack sink in further when its sharp end is down?
8. Did the chalk sink into the ice?

9. Did the wood sink into the ice?
10. Compare the prediction sheet you made at the beginning of the experiment with the actual results of the experiment.

Backyard Scientist solution to experiment.

Did you discover that the penny left its impression on the ice and you were able to see Lincoln's face in the ice? The penny was able to go all the way through the ice. By looking at the nickel very closely through the ice you saw that it looked the size of a half dollar. The washer went into the ice further when you pushed it in and also when the washer was on its edge rather than being flat. The thumb tack sank in further when its sharp end was down. The chalk and wood would not sink into the ice. Based on this experiment you have discovered that heavier and sharp objects sink in further. Why? You also discovered that those things that conduct heat well sank into the ice faster than those that do not conduct heat well.

Other fun investigations to try with this experiment would be to try putting hot pennies rather than cold pennies onto the ice to see which will sink first. Try putting cold washers on the ice and see what happens. Can you stop metal from sinking into the ice by putting something between the ice and metal? If you put the washer on the wood, will it make the wood sink in? Would the washer get cold? Will a pile of two or three washers sink in more than one washer? Which will sink in more, a pile of warm washers or a pile of cold washers? Explore the above possibilities and record your results.

FREEZING EXPERIMENT

Does the freezing rate of water change when something is added to the water?

Try the following Backyard Scientist experiment to discover the answer.

Gather the following supplies:

3 small plastic or paper cups (4 or 5 oz. size), water, rubbing alcohol, salt, spoon, pencil and paper, and a freezer or refrigerator with a freezer section.

CAUTION: *REMEMBER NEVER TO DRINK OR EAT ANYTHING YOU ARE EXPERIMENTING WITH.*

Start Experimenting.

1. Fill the 3 small cups ½ full with water. All cups must have the same amount of water in them.
2. Label the cups No. 1 water, No. 2 water and salt, and No. 3 water and alcohol.
3. Take the pencil and paper and make a chart for recording the results of this experiment. You are going to be writing down the results of this experiment each hour for three hours.
4. Now put a teaspoon of salt in the cup marked No. 2. Put a teaspoon of alcohol in the cup No. 3. Do not add anything to cup No. 1.
5. Place all cups in freezer but do not cover them.
6. Mark on your chart the exact time you put all three cups into the freezer.
7. Check the cups each hour for three hours. Based on your observations, write on your chart how well or how poorly each solution in the cup is freezing.

Can you answer the following questions from your observations?

1. After one hour were all the liquids in the cups freezing at the same rate? Which of the cups, if any, was the first to freeze? Did any of the cups not freeze at all?
2. Do step 1 again after two hours and then again after three hours. Be sure to record your observations on the chart.
3. How is the freezing rate of water affected by the addition of salt or alcohol?

Backyard Scientist solution to experiment.

Did you discover that after one hour the cup with only the water began to freeze? Ice was just beginning to form on the surface of the

water and alcohol mixture depending on how cold your freezer is. The cup containing the water and salt had not yet begun to freeze.

After two hours the cup containing water was frozen solid, the cup with alcohol and water was freezing and the cup containing the water and salt may now just begin to freeze, but will not become solid like the cup containing only water.

Certain chemicals can reduce the temperature at which water normally freezes (32° F. or 0°C.).

Alcohol is used to inhibit freezing in automobile radiators. Depending on the low temperatures in the area you live in, people add varying amounts of ethyl glycol, a form of alcohol, to their car radiators to keep them from freezing. If the radiator froze, it could crack, since water expands as it freezes.

Salt, or sodium chloride (NaCl) when added to water breaks down into sodium and chlorine ions. These ions prevent the water molecules from getting next to each other to form solid ice until the temperature is considerably below the normal freezing temperature. Lower than is possible to achieve in home freezers.

Suggestions for further experimenting. Try adding varying lesser amounts of salt to cups of water to determine the minimum amount of salt it takes to prevent freezing. Can other chemicals prevent freezing? Try using potassium chloride which is a common salt substitute used by people who must limit the intake of regular salt. It is available in the grocery store.

THINKING

CONGRATULATIONS! YOU HAVE ALMOST COMPLETED ALL THE EXPERIMENTS IN THIS BOOK. I HOPE YOU HAVE ENJOYED THEM AS MUCH AS I DID WHEN I PERFORMED THEM. BE SURE TO SEND IN FOR YOUR BACKYARD SCIENTIST CERTIFICATE. INFORMATION ON HOW TO GET IT IS ON PAGE 52 OF THIS BOOK.

For your last experiment I am giving you a thinking experiment. Have you ever done a thinking experiment before? Don't look at the solution until you have tried the experiment on your own. Have someone tape a piece of paper over the solution so you won't be tempted to look.

Gather the following supplies:

6 plastic 6 or 8 oz. glasses, colored or white cotton balls, labels for each glass, pen and paper.

CAUTION: *REMEMBER NEVER TO EAT OR DRINK ANYTHING YOU ARE EXPERIMENTING WITH.*

Start Experimenting.

1. Take the 6 glasses and write No. 1 on glass one, No. 2 on glass two, and so on until all six glasses are numbered.
2. Now line up the glasses in order from 1 to 6.
3. Take the cotton balls and put 6 cotton balls into the No. 1 glass, put 6 cotton balls into the No. 2 and the No. 3 glasses. You should now have cotton balls in glasses No. 1, No. 2 and No. 3.
4. Leave glasses Nos. 4, 5, and 6 empty.
5. The glasses should all be lined up in a row.
6. Here is your thinking exercise: You may touch and move only one glass. You are to change the line of glasses so that no empty glass is next to another empty glass and no full glass is next to another full glass.
7. Here is a clue. Re-read the directions and analyze what information is right there in the instructions.
8. Use your pen and paper to figure it out if you wish.
9. Remember, you only have to follow what is in the directions.

Can you answer the following questions from your observations?

1. What did the directions tell you to do?
2. What is not in the directions that you can do?
3. Are you missing the very obvious? Don't feel bad, most of us do.

Backyard Scientist solution to experiment.

The instructions allowed you to move one glass. No other restrictions were given. Thus you could have taken the cotton balls out of glass No. 2 and put them into the empty glass No. 5. Replacing the now empty glass No. 2 in the line of six glasses would give you a pattern of one glass full of cotton balls alternating with one empty glass, thus satisfying the instructions.

I would love to know how many of you got this without looking at the solution. Please write to me: Backyard Scientist, P.O. Box 16966, Irvine, CA 92713.

Now remember, keep experimenting and learning, and there are no limits to where your mind might travel or what you will be when you grow up.

Get Ready for More Exciting Hands-on Science Experiments in Other Backyard Scientist Books

Each award winning and best selling book contains different and stimulating hands-on science experiments...that work. These exciting experiments require supplies that are commonly found in the home or that are readily available at very low cost.

The Original Backyard Scientist and **Backyard Scientist, Series One** give the 4- to 12-year-old investigator an excellent introduction to chemistry, physics and the solid sciences.

Backyard Scientist, Series Three focuses the 4- to 12-year-old scientist on the life sciences.

Backyard Scientist, Series Four contains an exciting collection of hands-on science experiments that children of all ages will enjoy doing. It is an excellent resource for individual, family, group and classroom investigations. Many exciting aspects of chemistry and physics, are explored in these electrifying hands-on experiments.

Backyard Scientist, Exploring Earthworms With Me: Young scientists will learn to work with living animals as they sharpen their skills in the scientific process of observing, communicating, comparing, ordering, categorizing, relating, inferring and applying.

Backyard Scientist It's Like Magic Super Crystal Kit allows children to use the scientific method to explore the unique properties of the nontoxic (when used as directed), environmentally safe chemical contained in the kit. Using simple arithmetic, children will make scientific comparisons. So much learning and a lot of fun at the same time!

Get Your Official Backyard Scientist Certificate and Join the Backyard Scientist Club!

Just print your name and address on a slip of paper and state that you have completed all the experiments in the book. Include 52 cents in stamps and I will send you your official Backyard Scientist Certificate and enroll you in the Backyard Scientist Club. Also, The Backyard Scientist would like to know which experiments you liked best and why.

Write to: Backyard Scientist, P.O. Box 16966, Irvine, CA 92713

Backyard Scientist books are available from school supply stores, museum shops, toy stores, bookstores, and many catalogs of educational materials.